IMPROVING CLASSROOM MANAGEMENT

A plan that will reduce stress and benefit students

JIM SHAULIS

Author & Illustrator

Improving Classroom Management

First Edition

ISBN: 978-0-9891240-4-1

Jim Shaulis Publishing
Florida, USA

This book is dedicated to the devoted teachers who want to improve their classroom management.

Acknowledgments

Thanks and appreciation to the following:

- Cydelle Quinn, an incredible educator, for her encouragement and suggestions,

- My wonderful wife, Terry, for her willingness to listen and contribute,

- David Jones, a gifted teacher and administrator for his backing and support,

- And Kimberly Martin and her staff at Jera Publishing for their expertise.

Foreword

This book has been written to be as brief as possible. Reading it more than once and role playing the strategies would be beneficial. If you want further explanations, strategies, or tips read <u>Managing Student Behavior</u> (Jim Shaulis, 2024).

Contents

What Can I Do?

Your goal is to have your students like you and respect you. They are still developing and need both guidance and parameters. If not provided, they are likely to misbehave. Children who follow instructions are a joy to teach, which results in you being less stressed and the students being happier.

Any change takes extra time and work. You need to make a commitment. Your lessons and materials must be well planned ahead of time so you can devote your energy to your instructional delivery and classroom management.

If you can answer "Yes!" to the following questions, you have a good chance of creating a safe, happy, and productive learning environment.

1. Can you develop positive relationships with your students?

2. Can you greet each student at your entrance every day?

3. Will you use bell work to start each day?

4. Are you capable of managing your students while you teach them?

5. Can you remember to praise your students when it is earned?

6. Do you have the ability to improve your awareness – withitness?

7. Can you limit group punishment to only mild forms?

8. Can you teach procedures and turn them into routines?

9. Are you capable of creating a behavior plan and using it?

10. Can you be a calm enforcer?

11. Can you use positive talk when conferencing students and parents?

12. Are you a responsible, caring adult – a role model - rather than a friend?

1. Can you develop positive relationships with your students?

In years to come, your students may forget what you taught them, but they will always remember how you made them feel. (Paraphrased, Maya Angelou quote)

Students don't care how much you know until they know how much you care. (Paraphrased, Theodore Roosevelt quote.)

Without a foundation of a good relationship, students commonly resist rules and procedures along with the consequent disciplinary actions. (Marzano, Marzano, & Pickering, 2003, p. 41)

If the students like you, they will learn for you. (Mrs. Crotts, kindergarten teacher)

How do you show students that you care? See your students as individuals – not as a class such as third hour. Greet them every day, smile, use their names when addressing them, be a good listener, do whatever it takes to make them successful, etc. The list is endless.

The **number one variable** regarding classroom management is your teacher-student relationships. "***You have to earn the right to discipline.***" (Quote from a Nun who was a life-long educator)

2. Can you greet each student at your entrance every day?

Greeting students every day takes preparation. You must have your lessons ready to go and needed materials in place. As a favor to yourself, never leave school without being set for the next day. If coaching or family obligations require leaving early, either take work home or go to school early. There is a positive correlation between having a good day and being well prepared.

When you greet your students, give eye contact, smile, use appropriate physical contact, (shake hands, fist bump, high five, etc.) address them by their names, and if there is time, make a positive, personal comment. (Scott Ervin, 2022, pp. 72 – 73) This shows you care.

3. Will you use bell work to start each day?

Fred Jones recommends bell work to begin each day (2014, pp. 139 – 140). This gets the students into an academic frame of mind and provides the teacher with time to greet and take attendance. It must be self-directed and not last more than five minutes into the day's lesson. Here are some possible examples:

- Print this noun and draw a picture of it.

- Trace each of your spelling words two times.

- Solve as many of these problems as you can.

- List everything you know about _____.

- Read the first paragraph on page _____. Write what you think the author means.

- Study the graph on page _____. What facts can you summarize from it?

- Study your notes for today's test.

Elementary: individual folder work, review, brain teaser, partner work like flash cards, etc. Secondary: lesson launcher, review, define words, etc.

Of course you will discuss the students' work or provide the correct answers. No grades are given for bell work. You could add a bonus point to the daily averages for those who work hard at it.

What about the end of the day? Frequently teachers will permit their students to have "free time "when lessons end early. Keep this quote from Ruby Payne in mind (2005, DVD Module 6):

> *95% of all referrals are written during the first*
> *and last five minutes of the class.*

This time is an opportunity to review or check for comprehension: quiz, discussion, academic game, etc.

4. Are you capable of managing your students while you teach them?

Multitasking is not easy. If you watch a skilled teacher you may not even notice the subtle redirections that are given while they instruct their students. Here are some examples:

- The teacher pauses instruction to wait for quiet. <u>You **never** teach while students are talking.</u>

- While lecturing, the teacher walks near a potential disruptor. The distraction stops before it can gain momentum. Proximity is an excellent technique to squelch misbehaviors. Fred Jones states: *The most basic factor that governs the likelihood of goofing off in the classroom is physical distance from the teacher.* (2014, p. 30)

- The teacher places a hand on a student's desk as a warning: "Don't go there." No words are spoken - this is an up-close proximity.

- The teacher says, "Is that correct, Terry?" while instructing. A rhetorical question can bring a student back to focus.

- The teacher checks on students near an off-task student using peripheral vision to observe the student who might say "**What?**" if directly approached.

Skilled teachers always follow-up their subtle redirections to insure that the students are complying and to send the message to the class that they mean business. Two additional observations are usually sufficient. **Those who do not follow-up on their redirections are teaching in the "Danger Zone" which will result in the loss of control.**

Give all your students a front-row seat by circulating as much as possible during instruction. Also carefully plan the seating chart(s) separating the disruptive students.

Sometimes even a master teacher has to stop instruction for a moment to achieve compliance. Here are three examples of this:

- Teacher stops talking, raises a hand, and waits for silence. (Quiet signal)

- The teacher stops instruction, turns to the disruption, and "throws a whisper" saying the student's name. Others hear it, but because it isn't a loud calling out, it isn't perceived as a harsh demand. The teacher can even use a hand signal such as one of the following:

  - Finger to mouth = quiet

  - Twirling finger pointing down = turn around

  - Pointing toward the desk = get to work

  - Palm down = settle down

- The teacher stops talking, and slowly turns around in four movements: head, shoulders, waist, feet, taking approximately six seconds. This is done with hands at their sides and a <u>neutral expression</u>. (A smile conveys it is not serious and a mean look may prompt confrontation.) Nothing is said. The body language says it all. (Fred Jones, 2014, pp.187-90) This technique, "The Regal Turn", is powerful if not overused.

After the above strategies, the teacher <u>always</u> gives reinforcement even <u>before</u> compliance. Mouth a "Thank You," or give thumbs up. You could also do both.

This may sound unnecessary to you, but practicing the above by pretending to teach and redirect is a good idea. Just circulate around your empty room and envision a full class with a few students off task. Go through one of your lessons and practice each of the above strategies. Remember to do reinforcement after each redirection. This exercise will definitely be worth doing.

5. Can you remember to praise your students when it is earned?

Praising students for doing the right thing and giving a good effort is essential. Regardless of grade level, all students benefit from genuine praise.

Occasional group praise such as: "Class, you did a great job on your projects." is okay, but individual praise is more powerful. Younger students don't seem to mind when it is given publicly for others to hear. Older students in middle and high school tend to accept private praise better.

6. Do you have the ability to improve your awareness – withitness?

Some teachers just keep teaching regardless of their students' behaviors. This is sending the message to them that it is ok to talk and even "act out" during instruction. If this sounds vaguely familiar, you have to take a strong look at yourself. Teachers generally do this because of one of the following reasons:

- They have convinced themselves that there isn't time to stop instruction. The lesson must be covered.

- Their philosophy is that children will be children, and they will retain the information regardless of the disruptions.

- They are fearful of conflict.

- They are truly unaware.

Jacob Kounin was an educational theorist. He coined the term "withitness" – the ability to hear and see all. Successful teachers have withitness. So must you!

If you are stuck at the front of the room using technology, make frequent pauses to look over your shoulder to check on your students. You want to have the reputation that you have "eyes in the back of your head." (Note: There are tablets and remotes available that enable teachers to be away from the board.)

You must understand that the following is an absolute requirement for you to be successful:

Only instruct quiet students.

7. Can you limit group punishment to only mild forms?

It is better to miss a student who has misbehaved than to punish a child who was doing the right thing. Using your withitness, you will eventually catch the one(s) who don't comply.

Group punishment like loss of recess, canceling a privilege, assigning extra homework or writing sentences can ruin a teacher's likeability. Mild forms of group punishment can be helpful without alienating the innocent. Here are some examples:

- *We'll go to lunch when everyone is facing forward, quiet, and has hands at their sides.*

- *We'll begin when everyone is focused.*

- *I will dismiss the class when the room is clean.*

Don't continue to hold the whole class responsible. Just redirect those out of compliance and use consequences for them.

8. Can you teach procedures and turn them into routines?

A vast majority of behavior problems in the classroom are caused by the lack of procedures. (Wong & Wong, 2018, p. 140)

Anything you have your students do on a regular basis needs a procedure. It must be taught and practiced until it becomes a routine that is automatic. <u>The trick here is that anytime a procedure is not followed, you stop instruction and reteach it</u>. In the long run you will save time.

Procedures contribute to a productive learning environment. They provide structure for the students by eliminating confusion.

Two examples

- *Bobby, come back. How are you supposed to enter class? That's correct, quietly. Let's try it again.*

- *Everyone come back. The bell does not dismiss you. I do. Let's try it again.*

Here are some procedures that practically every classroom needs:

- How to enter class

- Quiet signal

- Headings for their class / homework

- How to hand in work

- What to do when their work is done

- Getting permission to get a drink or go to the restroom

- How to dismiss

The quiet signal is a major component of controlling a class and must be both taught and practiced. Have your students talk with a neighbor. You raise your hand. Encourage them to do the same. Time them to see how long it takes to achieve silence. It should be less than 5 seconds. (Kagan Trainers emphasize this during all of their workshops.)

There are too many procedures to make posters for each, but here are two that may be beneficial:

How to Enter Class	When my Work Is Done
1. Walk to assigned seat 2. Quietly take out text, agenda, homework, and supplies. 3. Place book bag behind desk. 4. Quietly complete bell work.	1. Complete make-up work. 2. Study notes, vocabulary, or flashcards. (If with partner, get approval.) 3. Do posted, bonus activity.

Wording will vary with grade levels.

9. Are you capable of creating a behavior plan and using it?

A behavior plan has three components: expectations, consequences, and rewards. The expectations drive everything you do every day. The consequences are there for when subtle redirections are not enough, and the rewards reinforce good behavior. The plan needs to be posted in a place for all to see.

A common outcome of not having a behavior plan is the teacher giving multiple redirections until he/she reaches a breaking point and writes a referral.

Expectations

You need to refer to your expectations on a regular basis: frequently for young children and as needed for older students. Possible frequencies:

- Three times per week for primary grades

- Twice per week for intermediate grades

- Once per week for middle grades (Mondays are best.)

- As needed and when deserving of praise for high school

Examples of use:

- Beginning of day/week: *Let's review our expectations.*

- End of day: *How did we do on our expectations today?*

- Referring to expectations that were followed: *Everyone came to class on time and immediately began the bell work. That's being both prompt and productive.*

Expectations are not wallpaper. They are a working document. Here are some possible examples:

Elementary

EXPECTATIONS

1. Be kind with words and actions.
2. Work and play safely.
3. Get permission to leave your seat.
4. Use indoor voices.
5. Always do your best.
6. Keep our classroom neat and clean.

Middle

EXPECTATIONS

1. Be kind to others.
2. Stay on task.
3. Keep hands, feet, and objects to self.
4. Respect all property.
5. Follow directions first time given.

High School

EXPECTATIONS

1. Be polite.
2. Be prompt.
3. Be prepared.
4. Be productive.

Consequences

Check your colleagues' consequences. They may fit you. They must be reasonable, sequential, administration approved, and <u>comfortable enough for you to use.</u>

Begin with an official warning that the student will earn when you decide there have been enough subtle redirections. A student only earns one warning. <u>Never</u> go back to subtle redirections. When do you begin consequences? It will not be the same for every student – it's individualized. Keep the following in mind:

- Is the student trying to comply?

- How long did the student comply before going off task again?

- Is the student capable of staying on task for long periods of time? (An accommodation or incentive may be needed.)

List every acceptable consequence you can. Place them in order from least to most severe. Decide how many and which ones you will use. The first is the warning and the last will be a referral to administration or counseling.

Once they are set, they will provide you with a sequential path to follow. Let the class know that if they earn #1, the next step is #2 and so on. An exception would be if there is a severe misconduct which would skip to a referral. Generally there is a fresh start each day. (Some schools use detentions which may continue for a day or two.)

CONSEQUENCES
1. Warning
2. 5 min. off recess/activity
3. 10 min. off recess/activity + 1:1 conference
4. In-class time out
5. Out-of-class time out + parent contact
6. Referral

CONSEQUENCES
1. Warning
2. Brief 1:1 conference
3. Seat of Opportunity
4. Alternative room + parent contact
5. Referral
Severe misbehaviors go directly to higher consequences.

When a student earns a 1:1, they know that as soon as the lesson is over (or after class) they will have a face-to- face talk with their teacher. If you use 1:1 conferences as a consequence, keep these suggestions in mind:

1. Keep a neutral expression.

2. Have the student face away from their peers. Talking in private (outside your entrance) is best.

3. Pretend that the parents are behind the student.

4. Begin with, "How can I help you? I don't want to see you earn anymore consequences." Or "I don't want anyone to get hurt."

5. Pause each time after you speak. It places the student into a "discomfort zone" to reflect. (Sarasota County Teacher, Rich Clay, coined the term)

6. Be sure they know what the correct behavior is.

7. Also, let them know what the next consequence is.

8. Always end with: "I know you will do better." This leaves the student with some dignity.

Here is an example of a possible 1:1 conference:

1. How can I help you? **Pause.**

2. Why did you do/say that? **Pause.**

3. Student's name, you are too nice of a person to act like this. **Pause.**

4. I don't want to see anyone hurt or you earning further consequences. **Pause.**

5. What is the next consequence? **Pause.**

6. What is the correct behavior? **Pause.**

7. Can you do that? **Pause.**

8. Student's name, I know you will do better.

Timeouts

"Seat of Opportunity" is sometimes used before an actual timeout. Explain to your class that it is not meant to embarrass anyone. It is simply a change of seat to remind the person to settle down so they don't earn any further consequences. If the teacher says a student's name and points to the desk, they should pick up their items and move to it (a desk off to the side). Participation is still allowed.

Timeouts are stricter. The student can be in the room, but does not participate. (Study carrels work great.) Post the following:

TIMEOUT

1. Stay seated
2. Be Quiet
3. Raise hand for help.

If placed out of the room, you must still have visual contact like a middle room with glass. Days of putting a student out in the hall and unsupervised are over.

If you have a colleague who is willing to do exchanges, you can use each other for alternative, room timeouts. (Some principals permit this. Some do not.) If you ever receive a student from another room you might say. "Hello, my name is _____. I'm sorry you are having a tough day. You are welcomed to my class as long as you follow the three rules." If the visitor disrupts your class, send them back, and the original teacher should write a referral.

"Time and Space Place" and "Cool Down Zone" are two of the names that have been used to describe timeout seats. Regardless of their monikers, they all have the same three rules.

SAMPLE PARENT NOTE

Oct. 16, 2025

Mr. and Mrs. Reynolds,

Today Grant earned the fourth consequence on our behavior plan – a parent note. Please encourage him to be a good listener during instruction and to raise his hand to contribute or ask a question.

I will send you a note next week to let you know how he is doing. I'm confident that he can do better.

Please sign below and have Grant return this note tomorrow. Your support is truly appreciated.

Thank you,

Mr. Shaulis

Mr. Shaulis, Social Studies Teacher

Parent/ guardian signature: _____ ___/___/___

Tip: Remind the student that you have copies of the parents' signatures in their cumulative folder. Also, when you hold parent-teacher conferences, you will be showing them copies of this letter.

Notice the following:

1. The student's misbehaviors are not listed. What the student needs to do is listed instead. It sounds less abrasive and the misbehaviors are understood.
2. The teacher has committed to a future progress report. This needs to be included in next week's lesson plan(s) or calendar so it is not forgotten.

Side note: Have you ever been in the grocery store when a parent with a basket full of goods says to their screaming child, "If you don't stop, I will take you home right now!"? Do they really mean what they say? Are they actually going to leave the cart and take the child home? Empty threats are useless. Don't be like this parent. Only say what you will do.

Rewards

Rewards are somewhat controversial. Some educators feel that rewards, such as: earning a good grade, correctly answering a question, or a smile and a pat on the back by their teacher, are sufficient. There are students, however, who don't possess as much inner motivation as others. Extra extrinsic rewards can make a difference for them.

REWARDS

1. Be proud.
2. Earn good grades.
3. Earn privileges:

The poster above shows two intrinsic rewards. Then #3 requires you to list privileges such as: a positive note to a parent, teacher's helper, line leader, academic game with a friend, computer time, , homework pass, permission to work with a partner, academic, game for the whole class, etc. Some elementary classes have treasure chest points, reward ladders, and other incentives for rewarding acts of kindness and outstanding efforts. A whole book could be written about rewards. Just don't overdo it.

Keep this in mind: *The best reward a child can earn is learning something new and your praise.* (Spencer Kagan quote)

10. Can you be a calm enforcer?

When you redirect a student or assign an earned consequence you should keep a <u>neutral expression</u> and speak with a calm voice. Remember to pretend that the student's parents are standing behind them. You are the adult – the professional.

If the situation becomes tense, remember these Fred Jones quotes (2014):

- *It takes one fool to backtalk. It takes two fools to make a conversation out of it.* (p.,210)

- *Emotions are contagious. You will get exactly what you give.* (p.168)

- *Calm is strength. Upset is weakness.* (p. 167)

Arguments don't generally last when one party is doing all the work. The upset person eventually begins repeating. When confronted with anger, Fred Jones recommends the following:

1. Breathe slowly as if watching TV. (Jones, 2014, p.168)

2. Relax your jaw muscles. (Jones, 2014, p.191)

3. Stay silent. (Jones, 2014, p. 211)

4. Focus on a point between their eyebrows – not their eyes. (Jones, 2007, video session 9)

5. Tune them out by thinking of a pleasant place or making a list of grocery items, names of candy bars, cars, etc. (Jones, 2007, video session 9)

6. Keep a calm expressionless face – a <u>neutral expression</u>.(Jones, 2014, p. 168)

Afterwards, you might make a statement like, "This is important to you. We'll talk after class." It will provide time for the student to settle down.

11. Can you use positive talk when conferencing students and parents?

Tell students what they should do – not what they are doing wrong. There will be exceptions, but positive talk is usually more easily accepted.

Non-example	Example
Dan, stop talking!	Dan, turn around and point your feet forward. Thank you.
Jen, stop combing your hair!	Jen, please use your break time to comb your hair. Thank you.

Positive talk with parents can also be used. You do want them on your side.

Non-example	Example
Lilly constantly talks and disrupts me during my instruction.	Lilly needs to be a good listener during instruction and to raise her hand to contribute.
Nick seldom comes to school with his homework, text, and supplies.	Nick needs to show you his homework, text, and supplies every night. Then he needs to place his book bag by the door so he remembers it.
Alex doesn't get along well with her classmates.	Alex needs to develop friendships.

12. Are you a responsible, caring adult – a role model - rather than a friend?

Whether you teach kindergarten or high school your students are watching. Your clothes, your expressions, your words, your actions, etc. are all examined. During the school year, teachers frequently spend more daytime with their students than their parents. You are a very important person. They don't need another friend. They need a responsible, caring adult - a role model. If a student is a loner, think of yourself as a counselor.

Two Interventions

1. Elementary

    <u>A reward strip can be used for **one or two** students at a time</u>. Using it for more will result in the teacher running around the room. The number of squares is determined by the students' needs. Each time a student successfully completes a lesson the teacher initials a square. When all the squares are initialed, the student earns a reward. Initials are never removed. They are simply not earned. Rewards have to be agreed upon in advance. Lunch in a special place with a friend, a positive note to the parents, computer time, academic game with a friend, etc. could be rewards. As the child improves the teacher increases the number of squares. Begin with five and work up to ten. Another alternative would be to have each box represent a half a day.

JS	JS	JS	JS	JS

2. Secondary

    <u>A tally card can be used with **one** student at a time</u>. It promotes self-awareness. Each time the student is redirected, a tally mark is recorded by either the student or the teacher. If the student does the recording, an index card is placed on his/her desk. Whenever you point to the desk, the student marks a tally. If the

teacher records, then an index card on a clipboard works well. At the end of class there is a brief conference discussing the card. Sometimes self-awareness and the conferencing will be enough. If not, a reward could be attached. Example: The teacher will reward if there are three or fewer tallies. As time goes on the number could decrease. Rewards have to be agreed upon in advance. Possible middle school rewards: lunch with a friend in a special place, computer time, work with a partner, positive note home, etc. High school is more limited: computer time, alternative assignment, positive parent contact, etc.

<u>Note</u>: With both of the above, a cooperative parent could be included. Sometimes the parent will even include a reward at home.

A Fresh Start

<u>If the school year has already begun, you need to reinvent yourself</u>. On a Friday, tell your students that when they return on Monday there will be a new behavior plan posted and they will have new seating assignments (ones that separate the non-compliant). Show them your expectations for entering your room. Don't tell them, but you will also look different when they come back. This author had a teacher who dressed up a bit, wore glasses rather than contacts, put her hair up and wore some low heels. After the class improved, she eventually went back to her usual, professional attire, but she kept up with all other changes.

<u>You get one chance at this</u>. Begin with calling back any student who doesn't enter the room correctly. Have them tell you what your expectations are for coming into your room. Have bell work posted on the board. After bell work, explain the new behavior plan or review the original one. Also begin immediately with excellent awareness using subtle redirections and your consequences if needed. It is a new day and you are a new teacher.

Do You Have the Fortitude to Change?

All of the information provided is important, but here are seven things you absolutely must accomplish:

1. Take the time to establish positive relationships with your students. <u>This is the most powerful strategy you have.</u>

2. <u>Always</u> greet your students at the door.

3. Place your procedures ahead of instruction until they become routines. Your quiet signal, a raised hand, is the most important one.

4. Have withitness - see all and hear all.

5. <u>Never</u> teach while students are talking.

6. <u>Always</u> follow-up your redirections to insure compliance.

7. Be a calm enforcer of your discipline plan.

References

1. Ervin, Scott. (2022). *The Classroom Manual.* Arlington, VA: ASCD

2. Jones, F.H. with Jones, P. & Jones J. (2014). *Tools for Teaching.* Santa Cruz, CA: Fredric H. Jones & Associates.

3. Jones, J.L. & Carpenter, L. (Producers) & Jones, F. (Director). (2007). *Tools for Teaching Video Toolbox* [Video Series, Disc 9/10, "Eliminating Backtalk"]. Phoenix, AZ.

4. Marzano, R.J. with Marzano, J.S. & Pickering, D.J. (2003*). Classroom Management That Works.* Alexandra, VA: ASCD.

5. Payne, R.K. (2005). *A Framework for Understanding Poverty.* Highlands, TX: aha! Process.

6. Wong, H. K. & Wong, R.T. (2018). *The first Days of School.* Harry K. Wong Publications, Inc.

About the Author

I have a bachelor and a master's plus 45 in education and administration. My teaching experience is 10 years at the elementary level and 20 years at the junior high / middle school level. I've been a K- 8 principal and acted as an assistant principal in a large middle school. The last nine years of my public school experience were as a teacher trainer in which I taught a variety of classes and went into all levels from Kindergarten to high school to observe, model and coach teachers. Since then I have been an educational consultant, during which time I wrote <u>Managing Student Behavior</u> and conducted many workshops. I've been an educator for over 54 years.

I am sure that I haven't seen everything, but I have witnessed a great deal. Hopefully, my experiences will benefit you.

Jim Shaulis

If you found *Improving Classroom Management* helpful, I would be grateful if you could take a moment to leave a review on Amazon. Simply scan the QR code below or visit www.amazon.com to share your thoughts. Thank you.

www.ingramcontent.com/pod-product-compliance
Lightning Source LLC
Chambersburg PA
CBHW071748020426
42331CB00008B/2223